T0070068

FACTS *for* FACTS

Steps for Discovering the real you

STEPHON KINCHEN

authorHOUSE®

AuthorHouse™
1663 Liberty Drive
Bloomington, IN 47403
www.authorhouse.com
Phone: 1 (800) 839-8640

Published by AuthorHouse   12/16/2016

ISBN: 978-1-5246-5485-6 (sc)
ISBN: 978-1-5246-5484-9 (e)

Chapter One

HELPING PEOPLE

If you don't believe in that much stuff, it is always good to know that there are helping people in life. Helping people are very good hearted people. Some people would say helping people would build a very good world where they could make life better. Those who help were put on this earth to help people. Also these people are known to have very good hearts, and they use those hearts to help people. Help is something that is good. It's a good thing that people in life help people, it inspires those people to help other people. Good help is the best help you can get. People should open their arms and accept help.

Some people think that if they help someone, it should come back to them in some sort of way. People say they help others because they remember when someone helped them, and therefore began to help others.

If you are not a helping person you will lose a lot of things in life that you could have had. You will definitely lose jobs due to the fact that your social skills are bad, and you don't have a good attitude. Help people at work when it's needed. People would say sometimes "once a good helping person, they will always be a helping person". Most people adore being a helping person, and receiving help because it makes them a strong person. Sometimes everyone needs help, whether it be helping someone with grocery bags, or giving them a few dollars in their pocket to buy things they need. Even if it's giving someone a ride to the store it is still helping that person out. People say that help is virtue, and it is true because helping people will make the world a better place. The better the world,

Chapter Two

WHY IS IT GOOD TO LIKE BEING HAPPY

It is a good thing to always be feel happy because being mad will only hold you down from being happy. Happiness brings joy, and good joy is the best joy. If you are a happy person, your kids will like you as a happy person. If you are always happy, but a sad or mad person, you may just need a little help in life. People should be happy due to the gratitude that they should have of just being alive. People should want to be happy, so when they go clothes shopping, and things like that, it will be fun because they are happy. People should live by God and the bible, and stay happy and positive to be able to help people who need some help. Then after you help those people in need of help, they will be fit to help other people along the way.

Happiness is a wonderful thing, but if you don't accept it, it will draw you to become a mad person that can barely maintain being happy and you choose t be sad. If you do accept being happy it will bring you joy and you won't have to worry about being mad or sad. You shouldn't stress in life, and want to feel mad or sad about something that happened to you. You should want to stay strong, and gain back your happiness.

As people know, church going people are very good hearted people who believe in people going to church to be saved from the streets and not living by God. A lot of people in life want to hang out with happy people, not mad people who they feel may want to cause them harm

Chapter Three

REASONS WHY YOU SHOULD ACCEPT GOOD THINGS IN LIFE

You should accept good things that you receive in life, because it will bring you more good things in life. If you don't accept good things you receive in your life, you will become a failure. Good things come to people in life that live the right way including living by our higher power father who is God. People's higher power who is God, will send those people gifts and blessings if they deserve them. Certain things and stuff by the living and accepting God they will receive those things in many different forms.

More reasons why people should accept good things they receive in life is because what you lose in life it's not well guaranteed to come back to them. It's easy in life to just accept good things you receive because you earned those things.

Some people in life don't accept some things they receive in life, because they care about how people might judge them. For example, someone might be wearing cheap clothing and look nice wearing them, but they rather wear expensive clothes because they are scared how someone look down on them. However, some people don't even accept the good part of their heart, and it leads them to failure due to having low self esteam that other people have helped them with. However, some people may have worked and received maybe 200 dollars a week, and they won't even accept that due to the fact that they believe they can get a better job working more hours when the job isn't guaranteed so they should just keep doing what was working for them to begin with.

Chapter Four

WHY IS IT A GOOD THING TO TAKE CARE OF PRIORITIES

It's a good thing to take care of your priorities so when you have kids they will grow up knowing that taking care of priorities is very important.

Priorities are responsibilities that almost everyone has, like keeping their house clean, going to work and things like that. Other priorities that people have are, going to work on time, and taking a shower, and brushing their teeth every day. These are major priorities that most people have, and most people are responsible enough to take care of them.

There is only one way to raise a child, and that is the right way. Kids should be taught to brush their teeth in the morning, after showering before making their

7

way to school. They should be neat and clean kids that clean up after themselves, which includes cleaning their rooms. If you as a parent help them with this, they will be responsible children.

Chapter Five

HOW NEW TECHNOLOGY IS AWESOME

There are a lot of new technology in the world today. Flat screen televisions are part of the new technology, and they are in almost all of the popular stores. WIFI is new technology that everyone seems to love today. WIFI comes in new phone data bases that are sold in stores. It's a good thing that WIFI is out now because everyone appreciates it, and they love using the service. It is so popular today to the point that people don't want to use internet service on their phones anymore. Sometimes if you do have internet on your phone it won't work, you have to use WIFI that comes with the phone. Some phones have built-in WIFI, and some you have to purchase from the phone company.

Touch screen laptops are in stores now with WIFI programmed into them. Some people think that if they have a nice laptop that they will be popular people. Laptops used to come without WIFI, but now they come with it programmed into it

In this world these days, technology has been updated in many ways. However laptop computers don't always have internet on them. Due to one of the new technology internet services called WIFI is popular to this world right now. It's high technology, and it is awesome. Just having a laptop these days, will make you a popular person if you have WIFI on it. As far as a cell phone goes, the updated ones have WIFI on them, and people love to use the service that they have on them. Also as far as technology, a new phone comes out every month and they all have WIFI on them, and people actually purchase them, and like

WHY ACCEPTING FAMILY AND FRIENDS IS IMPORTANT

Accepting your good family and friends is important because, everyone should accept good people who help them. Good family and good friends will help you out when you're down, sad, or mad. People should have gratitude for even having good family and friends. Some people wish to have good family and friends, and pray for these people also. Family and friends will keep you in good spirits. People may think that they don't need their family and friends when they do. These people will believe they can do everything on their own, and will live life perfectly refusing help. Friends and family will be there when you need money, rides to work, and even cook for you when you're hungry. They will also be there when you need someone to talk to for whatever reason.

There are many other ways a good friend or family can be there for you. When you need new clothes, and things like that, you can turn to your good family and friends which is a fact. When you cry and hurt mentally, the best people to turn to is your family and friends who will help you and they will show you that you have someone to turn to and make you feel better. They will also show you that you have someone to turn to in these drastic situations. It's a good thing to have supportive family and friends so you know that if anything happens, you have family and friends to call, even if it is to ask them if they have some Motrin, or Advil to cure your sickness. Overall, people should just be grateful for their loving family and friends.

Chapter Seven

DOCTORS CAN CURE YOU AND SAVE YOUR LIFE

Doctors can really save your life. When people get shot, stabbed, or something like that, doctors sometimes save their lives. Doctors can give you medications to help diagnosis to save your life. Doctors can even save your life if it took a long time to get to the emergency room in the hospital. They can also provide you with prescription medication to help you feel better, whether it a headache that you have, or a stomach ache, or a toothache. They are good people to have around because they can even bring people back to life. Even if the doctor can't bring you back 100%, they can hook you up to a life support machine and they can also bring you back to life through the life support machine. Doctors are trained to know how to operate on people, and make sure that they get the help that is needed. Doctors are the people that keep people alive.

Doctors went to school to learn how to fix major parts of the body. They can fix peoples arms and legs, and they can also do things like fix someone's foot. Doctors are people who you should look up to, because the work they can do is very awesome. If there were no doctors in this world, people would lose there lives each day. That is why it is awesome to have doctors on this earth.

If you want to depend on someone to save your life, you should depend on a doctor. Doctors have all types of medication that they can give you to prevent your chance of having a heart attack, and things like that.

They can also prescribe you medication to help you with diabetes, which would be an injection into your arm. A lot of people in this world have diabetes, and it is

Chapter Eight

KEEPPING A CLEAN HOUSE IS GOOD

Most people know that keeping a clean house is a priority, and some people keep their houses clean. Cleanliness is a must. People must know that the best way to live is by living in a clean house.

When you clean, you must wash the dishes' clean the counter with a good cleaning solution. You must also take the trash out so the house won't smell. The proper way to mop a floor is with bleach and Pinesol, unless you are allergic to Pinesol.

Another thing you need to do is clean all your walls with a cleaning solution. You must clean your bathroom, which includes cleaning your bathtub, the sink, the mirror, and the toilet. You also have to mop in the bathroom after you sweep, and you must clean the shower curtain so it does not attract dirt.

There are a lot of reasons why people should want a clean house' or apartment. One of the main reasons you should keep a clean house, or apartment, is because living sloppy will attract bugs and flies, and they won't leave sometimes until the house is clean.

Also you should use bleach during all of your cleaning. As a lot of people might know, the smell of bleach is very strong and it's made for cleaning and it's the best cleaning solution you can use sometimes. They say bleach kills germs, and it does, and it makes your house smell good.

Chapter Nine

PRAY TO GOD

God is everyone's higher power. Even the Muslim religion says that Allah is God. God is the person that put us on earth to live life. People pray to God, and God blesses them with the things that they have prayed for. People that pray and go to church are people that live by God. People that live by God are inspiring people that live and preach the word of God to get people to live by God day by day.

Some people might not be interested in praying and going to church, but if they get good help from people that are into praying to God and going to church, one day they will be interested and praying to God and going to church.

Our heavenly built this world so people can live well. He put banks on this earth so people have a place to put their saved money in the bank. He also put churches on earth so people have a place to go and praise God.

The Bible says that you must live by God, which means that you shouldn't live other than the Bible. Some people take that into consideration, and some people believe that it's ok to not live by God, which is ok by them, but it's not true because there is only one way to live and that is living by our heavenly father who is God.

It's not hard to live by God. All you have to do is accept God into your life, and you will honestly see that you were living better than before. God himself doesn't ask much from people, all he asks you to do is to pray and go to church, because it will benefit you mentally and physically, as well as cleanse your soul.

Chapter Ten

BUILDING TRUST FOR YOURSELF

One day everyone is going to see that they have to build trust for themselves. If you don't have trust in people it's really not good. Not having trust in people, people won't trust you. If you do have trust with people you will see that everyone will like you because you are a truthful person, and they can trust you. If your family and friends can't trust you there is only so much that they will do for you. People become to wonder why you can't trust someone after they already help them.

In relationships if one out of the two people can't be trusted, it's not a healthy relationship. People should build trust in one another by showing that they are loyal. People have to build trust for themselves, because you can only trust your family right away, not your friends.

When you meet new friends, there is only one way for you to show them that you are trustworthy, and that is by physically showing them that you will be there for them through good and bad situations.

If you get a job and you steal from that job, your manager might fire you because he feels like he can't trust you. In the same way, if you steal from your family and friends they will also feel like you can't be trusted after incidents like that. If you never steal from them why wouldn't they trust you? It will all turn out if you can trust some people, and you can't trust some people.

Chapter Eleven

PEOPLE SHOULD FEED THEIR BODIES VITAMINS

Feeding your body vitamins will make you very healthy and strong. Vitamins come in different types. There is vitamin D, A, B and C. Vitamins come in fruit juices and energy drinks. If you eat thing with vitamins in them your whole body can become strong. However, people who don't think that their body doesn't need vitamins, these are the people that find out later in life that they really did. This could be the reason they get toothaches, and headaches. These same people will then give their bodies vitamins, and find out they don't get headaches, and toothaches anymore.

Small children must be taught to take their vitamins, so they will grow up healthy children. When these children grow up they must also make sure their kids take vitamins just like they did.

People should have gratitude due to the fact that we have vitamins to put in our bodies to keep us strong, and healthy. You should make sure your body gets the proper amount of vitamins daily. If you take them daily, it will help your internal organs to work properly.

If you have children, and you don't teach them to give their bodies vitamins daily, how do you expect them to be healthy. You and your children should also drink plenty of water, because water has a lot of vitamins in it, and it will keep you healthy and hydrated. Most people know to drink a lot of water while being out in the sun to keep their throat from becoming dry, and to keep from getting dehydrated.

Chapter Twelve

HAVING PATIENCE

Having patience is a very good thing. If you have patience you are a very strong person. People must have patience for many reasons, like being able to work an eight hour work shift. If you don't have patience and rush your job, you might get fired which is nobody's fault but your own.

When you are driving your car, you have to have patience at a red light until it turns green. If you are driving behind a slower vehicle, you need to have patience and not follow to close or you may cause an accident.

You need to have patience in school to read your books and take tests to get a passing grade. Some people believe they don't have to study before tests, which is not true, because you need to study and do well on your tests so you can make it to the next grade.

If you are working on someone's car for them, you don't want to rush the job just to get the money because you might make the car worse than when you started. The best thing you can do in this situation is have the patience to fix it right the first time so you don't have to do it again.

When you are cooking, you don't want to have patience because if you hurry to get it done it may not be cooked all the way. If you turn up the heat to make it cook fast, you may burn it. Also if it is undercooked you may make someone sick.

When you are playing basketball you need to have patience, and focus on getting the ball in the basket.

Chapter Thirteen

PERFECT PEOPLE SAVES THE WORLD

What more can a person ask for when they have perfect people in the world on their side. Perfect people of the world are good hearted people who help others, and inspire them to never give up on life, and to be strong. Perfect people of the world give others money, buy them clothes, and give respect.

There are billions of who will help this world from falling apart. These people are angels who were born in this world, and grew up to help stop people from stealing, doing drugs, and hurting others. These people have strong beliefs that they live by. These people believe that if only a couple of people listen to them, that they can change and also become good citizens of the world.

Perfect people of the world will never let someone steal their dignity, or faith. Each day these people try their hardest to stop people from doing bad things, like committing crimes, and not caring about themselves. They say if you don't have respect for others. These are things people see in other people.

My definition of the perfect person is a person who tries to do good 100% of the time. Good people come from good people in this world.

Fathers and mothers who are perfect people of the world, taught their children how to be perfect and positive.

It's a good thing that perfect people run the world by being managers and supervisors at our work places. These people have a sense when to hire another good person at our workplace. They give others a chance even if their resume isn't that good. Once they get started working at the job they may start using bad habits and stealing, and talking back to the manager which will end up with them

Chapter Fourteen

EVERYONE HAS A FUTURE

You might not have the best future, but at least those people have something to look forward to which is their future. Some people have better luck than others, and futures to look forward to. Futures are something that keep people with the nice things in life.

A perfect person will always have a very bright future due to the good luck that they have built for themselves. You can build a good future by praising God, treating people with respect, and having a positive attitude that doesn't let other people bring them down. The person you were born to be, will be the person you grow up to be.

People should realize that living a negative lifestyle can turn it around to a positive lifestyle, which is the proper way to live. You don't have to stay around negative people, and become a negative person yourself. These are reasons why God doesn't give some people very good futures. God deals with all his children in a certain way. God will punish you for doing the negative things in life, like not living by God himself. So he figures he should let the good people have a future, and punish the bad ones until they decide to live as a good person.

These are the ways which God runs the world, which is in a way that is fair.

Chapter Fifteen

GETTING THE PROPER SLEEP

Getting the proper sleep at night is very important. Sometimes when you don't get the proper sleep, the next day you might feel sleepy and tired. It will be a bad thing if you have to go to work the next day because you might not have that much energy.

When you do get a proper night of sleep you will feel awake and refreshed, and you will be ready for work or whatever you have planned for the day. Your body will feel strong the way it's supposed to feel. All you will need to do in the morning is get a shower, and you feel good.

When people get the proper amount of sleep, which is eight hours, you should have all the energy you need. If you can take a nap during the day you will have even more energy. Taking naps leave you feeling very refreshed, and good. Naps are very healing to the body and the soul. I say that because when most people take naps, when they wake up they feel like they want to do something really fun.

Getting the proper amount of sleep should be a necessity, because when they don't they may wake up cranky. Some people even develop a bad attitude when they don't get the proper amount of sleep, and it brings on anger issues that they don't know how to deal with. Some people have an attitude, and they know they are cranky because they didn't get the proper amount of sleep. It's not fair to the people around them because they did nothing to these angry people. Due to all these anger problems, bad things can happen to innocent people, such as being

Chapter Sixteen

ACCEPTING GOOD THINGS IN LIFE

Some people in life don't accept some things they receive in life because they care how people may judge them. For example, someone might be able to wear cheap clothes and look nice wearing them, but they rather always buy expensive clothes, because they are scared of how someone would look at them, which is looking down on them. However, some people don't even accept the good part of their heart and it leads them to failure and to having low self-esteem that other people have already helped with them. However some people may have worked and receive $200 a week and they won't even accept that due to the fact that they believe they can get a better job, working more hours when they job isn't guaranteed. So they should of just kept what was working for them. Acceptance to people should be a honor in life for them because it's only so much luck you're going to have in life. Accepting things in life will make people feel better.

Chapter Seventeen

GOOD PEOPLE WILL BE THEIR FOR YOU

There are many other ways a good friend or family member will be there for you. When you need new clothes and things like that, who can you turn to? Your good family and friends which is a fact. When you cry and hurt mentally, the best people to turn to is your family and friends who will help you and make you feel better and they will show that you have someone to turn to in these drastic situations. It's a good thing to have supportive family and friends so you know that if anything happens you have family and friends to call, even if it's just to ask them if they have some Motrin or Advil to cure your sickness. Overall people should just be grateful for they have loving family and friends. A family with friends should just want to be a good family and live day by day in good spirits. They shall be strong and don't let anyone put them don mentally. The good family should work together and help the world where someone can become a friend to the family and have supportive help. And a lot of love.

Chapter Eighteen

LIVING DIRTY ISN'T CLEAN

Living sloppy and dirty will attract different types of bugs and flies and they won't leave sometimes until your house is clean. Also you should use bleach during all of your cleaning. As a lot of people might know, bleach is very strong and it's made of cleaning and it is the best cleaning solution you can use sometimes. When you smell the smell of belach, you can tell that is a good cleaner. They say bleach kills germs, which it does and it makes your hose smell good. If you are not a clean person, people won't even want to be around you. You might be a clean person because if you have kids and you're not a clean person, how do you expect your kid to be a clean person. That's why you must be a good person. You must teach your kids to be clean and to be responsible and to take care of responsibilities and to know what's right in this matter, which is being a clean, neat problem. It is a true fact that people must be a clean problem and never dislike being clean.

Chapter Nineteen

DOCTOR CAN SAVE YOUR LIFE

Doctors went to school to learn how to fix major parts in people's bodies. Doctors can fix peoples' arms and legs and they can also do things like fix someone's foot. Doctors are people who people should look up to because the work they can do is very awesome. If there were no doctors in this world, a lot of people would lose their lives by the day, That's why it is awesome to have doctors on this earth. If you want to depend on someone to save your life, you should depend on a doctor. However doctors have all types of medication that they can give you to lower your chance of catching heart aches and things like that. They can also prescribe you meds to help you with Diabetes, which will be an injection in my arm. A lot of people in his world have Diabetes and it definitely is not a good thing. So that's why there are doctors around to give them people meds and make sure that they get the proper services from the doctors that they need.

Chapter Twenty

TRUST WORTHY PEOPLE

If you get a job and you steal from the job, your manager might fire you because he feel like he can't trust you. In the same way, if you steal from your family and friends they will also probably feel like they can't trust you after incidences like that. But if you never steal from them why wouldn't they trust you. If all turns out in life that you can trust some people and you can't trust some people. Basically non-trustworthy people need help if you show them and tell them right way to live, which is being able to be trust, maybe those non trustworthy people will stop stealing and lying and become trustworthy. Sometimes people just need help, maybe so people are not trust worthy because they were never taught to be trust worthy. Overall it's not that people are bad people, it's just that these people might just needed a helping hand to be taught how to live like good people live. They are probably always needing someone to help them and they were just scared to ask for help. However some people rat. Live in denial rather than live by God. Some people believes that its okay to not live by God which is okay to them. But it's not true because there's only one way to live and that's living by the heavenly father who is God. Its hard to live by God, all you have to do is accept God into your life and you will honestly see that you are living better than how you were living before. God himself doesn't ask for much from people. He just asks you to pray and go to church because it will benefit you mentally and physically and will clean your soul. You should want to be saved so you always will know that God is with you. Some people get baptized and stop doing things that they were doing before, like selling drugs or breaking the law and not caring about the law. Once they are scared, most people cry and try to be happy that they finally are living by God and it makes them feel good. They know they will always be blessed by God. Also one day they can relate to people don't believe and help them.

Chapter Twenty One

VITAMINS HELP YOU

People should be glad and have gratitude due to the fact that we have vitamins to make use strong, healthy people. You should make sure your body gets the proper amount of vitamins daily. If you do that your insides will work accurately like they're supposed to. If not your liver will not work right, because if you don't give it the proper vitamins. You shouldn't only give your body vitamins sometimes you must do it everyday. And if you don't give your body vitamins every day and only sometimes, then your insides will only work properly maybe 50% of the time which is not up to standards. If you have children and don't teach them to give their bodies vitamins, how do you expect them to be healthy people who take and put vitamins in their bodies daily. You should also and your children must drink cold water because water will also make you healthy because your body needs water for the vitamins. That's in water and water will also keep you hydrated. Most people know that you must drink a lot of water because you throat will be very dry and for some people they will probably faint being under the sun dehydrated.

Printed in the United States
By Bookmasters